AF664166

JOURNALISM FOR WOMEN

A PRACTICAL GUIDE

SALMON BOOKS

JOURNALISM FOR WOMEN

A PRACTICAL GUIDE

E.A. Bennett

SALMON BOOKS

Chennai NewDelhi

Honour Copyright
&
Exclude Piracy

This book is protected by copyright. Reproduction of any part in any form including photocopying shall not be done except with authorization from the publisher.

SALMON BOOKS

ISBN 9789349032736 Salmon Books

All rights reserved
Printed and bound in India

No. 44, Nallathambi Street,
Triplicane, Chennai 600 005

MJP 103
© Publishers, 2025

Publisher **C. Janarthanan**

PUBLISHER'S NOTE

The legacy of a country is in its varied cultural heritage, historical literature, developments in the field of economy and science. The top nations in the world are competing in the field of science, economy and literature. This vast legacy has to be conserved and documented so that it can be bestowed to the future generation. The knowledge of this legacy is slowly getting perished in the present generation due to lack of documentation.

Keeping this in mind, the concern with retrospective acquiring of rare books has been accented recently by the burgeoning reprint industry. Salmon Books is gratified to retrieve the rare collections with a view to bring back those books that were landmarks in their time.

In this effort, a series of rare books would be republished under the banner, "Salmon Books". The books in the reprint series have been carefully selected for their contemporary usefulness as well as their historical importance within the intellectual. We reconstruct the book with slight enhancements made for better presentation, without affecting the contents of the original edition.

Most of the works selected for republishing covers a huge range of subjects, from history to anthropology. We believe this reprint edition will be a service to the numerous researchers and practitioners active in this fascinating field. We allow readers to experience the wonder of peering into a scholarly work of the highest order and seminal significance.

Salmon Books

Contents

Chapter I

THE SECRET SIGNIFICANCE OF JOURNALISM

For the majority of people the earth is a dull planet.

It is only a Stevenson who can say: "I never remember being bored;" and one may fairly doubt whether even Stevenson uttered truth when he made that extraordinary statement. None of us escapes boredom entirely: some of us, indeed, are bored during the greater part of our lives. The fact is unpalatable, but it is a fact. Each thinks that his existence is surrounded and hemmed in by the Ordinary; that his vocations and pastimes are utterly commonplace; his friends prosaic; even his sorrows sordid. We are (a few will say) colour blind to the rainbow tints of life, and we see everything grey, or perhaps blue. We feel instinctively that if there is such a thing as romance, it contrives to exhibit itself just where we are not. Often we go in search of it (as a man will follow a fire-engine) to the Continent, to the Soudan, to the East End, to the Divorce Court; but the chances are a hundred to one against our finding it. The reason of our failure lies in our firm though unacknowledged conviction that the events *we* have witnessed, the persons *we* have known, are *ipso facto* less romantic, less diverting, than certain other events which we happen not to have witnessed, certain other persons whom we happen not to have known. And such is indubitably the case; for romance, interest, dwell not in the thing seen, but in the eye of the beholder. And so the earth is a dull planet--for the majority.

Yet there are exceptions: the most numerous exceptions are lovers and journalists. A lover is one who deludes himself; a journalist is one who deludes himself and other people. The born journalist comes into the world with the fixed notion that nothing under the sun is uninteresting. He says: "I cannot pass along the street, or cut my finger, or marry, or catch a cold or a fish, or go to church, or perform any act whatever, without being impressed anew by the *interestingness* of mundane phenomena, and without experiencing a desire to share this impression with my fellow-creatures." His notions about the qualities of mundane phenomena, are, as the majority knows too well, a pathetic, gigantic fallacy, but to him they are real, and he is so possessed by them that he must continually be striving to impart them to the public at large. If he can compel the public, in spite of its instincts, to share his delusions even partially, even for an hour, then he has reached success and he is in the way to grow rich and happy.

* * * * *

We come to the secret significance of journalism:--

Life (says the public) is dull. But good newspapers are a report of life, and good newspapers are not dull.

Therefore, journalism is an art: it is the art of lending to people and events intrinsically dull an interest which does not properly belong to them.

This is a profound truth. If anyone doubts it, let him listen to a debate in the House of Commons, and compare the impressions of the evening with the impressions furnished by the parliamentary sketch in his daily paper the next morning. The difference will be little less than miraculous. Yet the bored observer of the previous night will find in the printed article no discrepancies, no insidious departures from sober fact; and as he reads it, the conviction will grow upon him that his own impressions were wrong, and that after all a debate in the House of Commons is a remarkably amusing and delightful entertainment. If the newspapers ceased to report the proceedings of Parliament, the uncomfortable benches of the Strangers' Gallery would for ever remain empty, simply because the delusion which now fills them nightly during the session would die for lack of sustenance. Again, take the case of the amiable feminine crowds which collect upon the Mall whenever Her Majesty holds a Drawing Room at Buckingham Palace. What has induced them to forsake lunch and the domestic joys in order to frequent that draughty thoroughfare? Nothing but accounts which they have read in vivacious newspapers of the sights to be seen there on these state occasions. They go; they see; they return fatigued and privately disappointed, with a vague feeling that some one has misled them. But with the arrival later in the afternoon of the vendor of special editions, they begin to be reassured. Under the heading "To-day's Drawing Room," they encounter a description of incidents which they themselves have witnessed. The sweet thought crosses their minds: "Perhaps that was written by the curious woman with eye-glasses who stood near to me;" and by the time dinner is over nothing would persuade them that the Mall on Drawing Room day is not one of the most interesting places in the world.

So the journalist continues to gain a livelihood by forcing his rosy fallacies upon the weary world.

* * * * *

In order to substantiate further the proposition that the art of journalism is the art of lending interest to people and events intrinsically dull, let me draw attention to the treatment accorded by editors to those rare trifles of information which by general agreement are not in themselves dull. Such an item, a jewel of its kind, was the following: I copy it as it was allowed to appear in an evening newspaper justly renowned for enterprise, talent, and imagination, under date 16th January, 1897:

"While walking in the Park at Tsarskoe Selo the Tsar beckoned to a gardener. The man hastened to obey, but a guard, thinking he was running up to attack the Emperor, shot him dead.

"His Majesty was deeply affected by the occurrence."

Observe the stark nakedness of it. There is no decorative treatment here, no evidence of an attempt to impress upon the report the individuality of the paper. The Editor rightly divined that the simple, splendid tragedy of the event offered no opportunity for a display of his art. His art, indeed, could have nothing to do with it. If all news were of a similar quality, the art of journalism, as it exists at present, would instantly expire, and a new art would arise to take its place, though what the nature of that new art would be, it is hazardous to guess. One may, however, assert that journalism in its highest development will only thrive so long and so far as the march of events continues, in the eyes of the majority, to be a dull, monotonous and funereal procession. The insensible hack may trust himself to present attractively an occurrence or a man that all the world concedes to be inherently attractive; but it needs a heaven-born artist, trained in the subtleties of his craft and gifted with the inexhaustible appreciative wonder of a child, to deal finely and picturesquely with, say, bi-metallism or the Concert of Europe.

* * * * *

And how to create interest where interest is not? Alas, no dissertation and no teacher can answer the question. As in other arts, so in journalism, the high essentials may not be inculcated. It is the mere technique which is imparted. By a curious paradox, the student is taught, of art, only what he already knows. Anyone can learn to write, and to write well, in any given style; but to see, to discern the interestingness which is veiled from the crowd--that comes not by tuition; rather by intuition.

The best treatise on art can only hope:--

1. To indicate the lines of study and training which should be pursued in order to acquire the measure of mechanical accomplishment necessary to the right using of the artistic faculty.
2. If the artistic faculty exists but is dormant, to awaken it by means of suggestion; and having awakened it, to show how it may be properly excited to the fullest activity of which it is capable.

This book is an attempt to do these things, for women, in the art of journalism.

Chapter II

IMPERFECTIONS OF THE EXISTING WOMAN-JOURNALIST

Despite a current impression to the contrary, implicit in nearly every printed utterance on the subject, there should not be any essential functional disparity between the journalist male and the journalist female. A woman doctor (to instance another open calling) is rightly regarded as a doctor who happens to be a woman, not as a woman who happens to be a doctor. She undergoes the same training, and submits to the same tests, as the young men who find their distraction in the music-halls and flirt with nurses. Her sex is properly sunk, except where it may prove an advantage, and certainly it is never allowed to pose as an excuse for limitations, a palliative for shortcomings. Least of all is she credited (or debited) with any abnormality on account of it. But towards the woman journalist our attitude, and her own, is mysteriously different. Though perhaps we do not say so, we leave it to be inferred that of the dwellers in Fleet Street there are, not two sexes, but two species--journalists and women-journalists--and that the one is about as far removed organically from the other as a dog from a cat. And we treat these two species differently. They are not expected to suffer the same discipline, nor are they judged by the same standards. In Fleet Street femininity is an absolution, not an accident. The statement may be denied, but it is broadly true, and can easily be demonstrated.

Such a condition of affairs is mischievous. It works injustice to both parties, but more particularly to the woman, since it sets an arbitrary limit to healthy competition, while putting a premium on mediocrity. Is there any sexual reason why a woman should be a less accomplished journalist than a man? I can find none. Admitted that in certain fields--say politics--he will surpass her, are there not other fields in which she is pre-eminent, fields of which the man will not so much as climb the gate? And even in politics women have excelled. There are at least three women-journalists in Europe to-day whose influence is felt in Cabinets and places where they govern (proving that sex is not a bar to the proper understanding of *la haute politique*); whereas the man who dares to write on fashions does not exist.

* * * * *

That women-journalists as a body have faults, none knows better than myself. But I deny that these faults are natural, or necessary, or incurable, or meet to be condoned. They are due, not to sex, but to the subtle, far-reaching effects of early training; and the general remedies, therefore, as I shall endeavour to indicate in subsequent chapters, lie to hand. They seem to me to be traceable either to an imperfect development of the sense of order, or to a certain lack of self-control. I should enumerate them thus:--

First, a failure to appreciate the importance of the maxim: Business is business. The history of most civil undertakings comprises, not one Trafalgar, but many; and in journalism especially the signal *Business is business*--commercial equivalent of *England expects*--must always be flying at the mast-head. *On ne badine pas avec l'amour*--much less with a newspaper. Consider the effects of any lapse from the spirit of that signal in a profession where time is observed more strictly than in pugilism, where whatever one does one does in the white light of self-appointed publicity, where a single error or dereliction may ruin the prestige of years! Consider also the rank turpitude of such a lapse! Alas, women frequently do not consider these things. Some of them seem to have a superstition that a newspaper is an automaton and has a will-to-live of its own; that somehow (they know not how) it will *appear*, and appear fitly, with or without man's aid. They cannot imagine the possibility of mere carelessness or omission interfering with the superhuman regularity and integrity of its existence. The simple fact of course is that in journalism, as probably in no other profession, success depends wholly upon the loyal co-operation, the perfect reliability, of a number of people--some great, some small, but none irresponsible.

Stated plainly, my first charge amounts to this: women-journalists are unreliable as a class. They are unreliable, not by sexual imperfection, or from any defect of loyalty or good faith, but because they have not yet understood the codes of conduct prevailing in the temples so recently opened to them. On the hearth, their respect for the exigencies of that mysterious *business* is unimpeachable; somehow, admittance to the shrine engenders a certain forgetfulness, Or perhaps it would be kinder and truer to say that the influences of domesticity are too strong to be lightly thrown off. For commercial or professional purposes these influences, in many cases, could not well be worse than they are. Regard, for a moment, the average household in the light of a business organisation for lodging and feeding a group of individuals; contrast its lapses, makeshifts, delays, irregularities, continual excuses, with the awful precisions of a city office. Is it a matter for surprise that the young woman who is accustomed gaily to remark, "Only five minutes late this morning, father," or "I quite forgot to order the coals, dear," confident that a frown or a hard word will end the affair, should carry into business (be it never so grave) the laxities so long permitted her in the home?

I would not charge the professional woman, as I know her, with any consistent lack of seriousness. On the contrary, she is in the main exquisitely serious. No one will deny that the average girl, when she adopts a profession, exhibits a seriousness, an energy, and a perseverance, of which the average man is apparently incapable. (It is strange that the less her aptitude, the more dogged her industry.) The seriousness of some women in Fleet Street and at the Slade School must be reckoned among the sights of London. It seems almost impossible that this priceless intensity of purpose should co-exist in the same individual with that annoying irresponsibility which I have endeavoured to account for. Yet such is the fact. Scores of instances of it might be furnished; let one, however, suffice. Once there was a woman-journalist in the North of England who wrote to a London paper for permission to act as its special correspondent during the visit of some royal personages to her town. The editor of the paper, knowing her for an industrious and conscientious worker and a good descriptive writer, gave the necessary authority, with explicit information as to the last moment for receiving copy. The moment came, but not the copy; and the editor, for the time being a raging misogynist (for he had in the meanwhile publicly announced his intention to print a special report), went to press without it. The next day, no explanation having arrived, he dispatched to his special correspondent a particularly scathing and scornful letter. Then came the excuse. It was long, but the root of it amounted to exactly this: "I was so knocked up and had such a headache after the ceremonies were over, that I really did not feel equal to the exertion of writing. *I thought it would not matter.*" Comment would be inartistic. The curious thing is that the special correspondent was an editor's wife.

* * * * *

Secondly, inattention to detail. Though this shortcoming discloses itself in many and various ways, it is to be observed chiefly in the matter of literary style. Women enjoy a reputation for slipshod style. They have earned it. A long and intimate familiarity with the manuscript of hundreds of women writers, renowned and otherwise, has convinced me that not ten per cent of them can be relied upon to satisfy even the most ordinary tests in spelling, grammar, and punctuation. I do not hesitate to say that if twenty of the most honoured and popular women-writers were asked to sit for an examination in these simple branches of learning, the general result (granted that a few might emerge with credit) would not only startle themselves but would provide innocent amusement for the rest of mankind. Of course I make no reference here to the elegances and refinements of written language. My charge is that not the mere rudiments are understood. Even a lexicographer may nod, but it surely requires no intellectual power surpassing the achievement of women to refrain from regularly mis-spelling some of the commonest English words. The fact that there are niceties of syntax which have proved too much for great literary artists, does not make less culpable a wilful ignorance of the leading grammatical rules; yet the average woman *will* not undergo the brief drudgery of learning them. As for punctuation, though each man probably employs his own private system, women are for the most part content with one--the system of dispensing with a system.

These accusations, I am aware, have no novelty. They are time-worn. They have been insisted upon again and again; but never sufficiently. And now the accusing sub-editors and proof-readers seem to have grown weary of protest. They suffer in silence, correcting as little as they dare, while all around are appearing women's articles, which, had their authors been men, would either have met with curt refusal or been returned for thorough revision.

The root of the evil lies, as I think, in training. The female sex is prone to be inaccurate and careless of apparently trivial detail, because that is the general tendency of mankind. In men destined for a business or a profession, the proclivity is harshly discouraged at an early stage. In women, who usually are not destined for anything whatever, it enjoys a merry life, and often refuses to be improved out of existence when the sudden need arises. No one by taking thought, can deracinate the mental habits of, say, twenty years.

But some women are as accurate and as attentive to detail as the most impeccable man, while some men (such as have suffered in training) present in these respects all the characteristics usually termed feminine. Which shows that this question at any rate is not one to be airily dismissed with that over-worked quotation: "Male and female created he them."

* * * * *

Thirdly, a lack of restraint. This, again, touches the matter of literary style. Many women-writers, though by no means all, have been cured of the habit of italicising, which was the outcome of a natural desire to atone for weakness by stridency. (Every writer, of whatever sex, must carry on a guerilla against this desire.) It is useless, however, to discipline a vicious instinct in one direction, if one panders to it in another. Women have given up italics; but they have set no watch against over-emphasis in more insidious forms. And so their writing is commonly marred by an undue insistence, a shrillness, a certain quality of multiloquence. With a few exceptions, the chief of whom are Jane Austen and Alice Meynell, the greatest of them suffer from this garrulous, *gesticulating* inefficacy. It runs abroad in *Wuthering Heights* and *Aurora Leigh* and *Sonnets from the Portuguese*. And George Eliot, for all her spurious masculinity, is as the rest. You may trace the disease in her most admired passages. For example:--

"It was to Adam the time that a man can least forget in after life, --the time when he believes that the first woman he has ever loved betrays by a slight something--a word, a tone, a glance, the quivering of a lip or an eyelid--that she is at least beginning to love him in return. The sign is so slight, it is scarcely perceptible to the ear or eye--he could describe it to no one--it is a mere feather-touch, yet it seems to have changed his whole being, to have merged an uneasy yearning into a delicious consciousness of everything but the present moment." (*Adam Bede*, p. 187.)

Observe here the eager iteration of the woman, making haste to say what she means, and, conscious of failure, falling back on insistence and loquacity. Exactly the same vehement spirit of pseudo-forcefulness characterises women's journalism to-day. And the worst is that these tactics inevitably induce formlessness and exaggeration; the one by reason of mere verbiage, the other as the result of a too feverish anxiety to be effective.

I submit that this lack of restraint shown by women writers as a class is due (like other defects) less to sex than to training. The value of restraint is seldom inculcated upon women. Indeed, its opposites--gush and a tendency to hysteria--are regarded, in many respectable quarters, as among the proper attributes of true womanliness; attributes to be artistically cultivated. When at length the principles on which women are brought up come to be altered, then this fault (and the others which I have mentioned) will disappear. In the meantime much can be done in individual cases by suitable moral and intellectual calisthenics.

Chapter III

THE ROADS TOWARDS JOURNALISM

More women long and strive to be journalists than by natural gifts are fitted for the profession. By itself, the wish is no evidence of latent capacity. Such desire may be induced by the need to earn a livelihood; or by the peremptory impulse to do *something* which drives forward so many women to-day; or perhaps through conversing with an enthusiastic journalist; or by printed statements as to the incomes and influence of certain famous members of the craft; or by the mere glamour which surrounds the newspaper life; or in forty other ways. The practice of journalism does not demand intellectual power beyond the endowment of the average clever brain. It is less difficult, I should say, to succeed moderately in journalism than to succeed moderately in dressmaking. Any woman of understanding and education, provided she has good health and the necessary iron determination, can become a competent journalist of sorts if she chooses to put herself into hard training for a year or two--and this irrespective of natural bent. Yet even so, I would recommend you, unless you are assured of a genuine predisposition towards it, to find another and less exhausting, less disappointing occupation than journalism. For it will surely prove both exhausting and disappointing to those whose hearts are not set fast upon it.

But how are you, the woman who desires to be a journalist, to ascertain whether you have that genuine predisposition, those natural gifts which will renew your strength and take away the bitterness of disappointments? You may come some way towards deciding the point by answering these three questions:--

1. Are you seriously addicted to reading newspapers and periodicals?
2. Does the thought regularly occur to you, apropos of fact or incident personally observed: "Here is 'copy' for a paper"?
3. Have you the reputation among your friends of being a good letter-writer?

If you cannot reply in the affirmative to two of these queries, then take up pokerwork, or oratory, or fiction, or nursing, but leave journalism alone. If by good fortune you are able to say "Yes" to all three of them, you may go forward rejoicing, for only perseverance will be necessary to your success; you are indeed "called."

* * * * *

There are several ways of entering upon journalism. One is at once to found or purchase a paper, and thus achieve the editorial chair at a single step. This course is often adopted in novels, sometimes with the happiest results; and much less often in real life, where the end is invariably and inevitably painful.

Another way is to buy the sub-editorship of a third-rate paper, by subscribing towards its capital. By such a transaction one gains experience, but the cost is commonly too dear.

Another way is to possess friends of high influence in the world of journalism, who will find for one a seat in a respectable office; an office where one will be in a position to learn everything without pecuniary risk, and where one can look forward to earning a salary within a reasonable time. The sole objection to this method is that it is usually quite impracticable.

Another way is to learn shorthand and the use of the typewriter, and so obtain an editorial secretaryship. An editor's secretary has every opportunity of conning the secrets of the profession, and it is her own fault if she is not soon herself a journalist.

But the time-honoured, the only proper way of entering upon journalism is to become what is called an "outside contributor." The outside contributor sends unsolicited paragraphs and articles to papers, on the chance of acceptance. By dint of a thousand refusals, she learns to gauge the public, which is the editorial, taste, and at length, fortified by many printed specimens of her work and a list as long as your arm of the various publications for which she writes, she is able to demand with dignity a position (in the office or out of it, as her tastes lie) on the staff of some paper of renown. Some journalists are so successful as outside contributors--writing when, how, and for whom they choose--that they would scorn the offer of any regular appointment; but such are rare.

Chapter IV

THE ASPIRANT

When you have decided to become an outside contributor you are entitled to call yourself by the proud title of "journalistic aspirant."

The procedure of the aspirant is usually this:--

She casts about for a subject on which to write, and according to her temperament and circumstances she will certainly choose one of six things:--"A Spring Reverie" (or it may be "An Autumn Reverie," as the time of year suits); or "Elsie, a character sketch" (describing one of those insufferably angelic women whom happily God never made); or "Hints on Economy in Dress"; or "My First Bicycle Ride"; or an exposure of the New Woman; or, lastly, a short story, probably styled "An Incident." and beginning: "Enid Anstruther had come to the end of her resources. As she sat by the fire that winter afternoon, the glow of the red coal playing on her soft brown hair, she reflected with a grim smile that," &c., &c.

The aspirant, left to herself, never goes beyond these six topics for her first venture.

Having written the thing, she copies it out in a hand as fair as she can compass (or, if she can afford the expense, gets it typewritten)--on one side of the paper only. She has read somewhere that manuscripts should be on one side of the paper only, and that they have a better chance of acceptance if typewritten. Next she stitches the sheets together, as a rule with black cotton; occasionally she uses a safety-pin for safety. Then she composes a pretty letter to the editor of the paper with which she happens to be most familiar, telling him that she is anxious to make a little money (though not dependent on her earnings for a livelihood), and hopes he will come to a decision on her article at his earliest convenience; she adds that she has always admired his journal, and would esteem it a great honour to be counted among his contributors.

She has previously determined to keep the whole affair a profound secret, but at the last moment she cannot refrain from showing the production, in strict confidence, to some near and dear one. This person either pronounces it to be really splendid, or damns it with a polite sneer; but whatever the event, her own golden opinion of her work is confirmed. In the act of dispatching the missive she suddenly remembers that the correct thing is to send a stamped envelope for return; she does so, only the envelope which she encloses is usually much too small to hold the manuscript.

So the article goes forth. A few days pass, and the aspirant is beginning to meditate upon the best manner of spending the money to be received for it, when lo! it returns....

* * * * *

Needless to say, the aspirant has set about the difficult business of becoming an outside contributor in quite the wrong way. Before daring to enter upon the writing of an article, it is needful that she should, in particular, make a study of four important subjects:--

1. The distinguishing characteristics, policy, and general tone of all the leading dailies, weeklies, and monthlies.
2. Spelling.
3. Grammar.
4. Composition, including punctuation. I will deal briefly with these four.

1. The object of the journalistic aspirant is to supply a demand. But in order successfully to supply a demand, it is necessary to know with some exactitude the nature of that demand. Of what use to send stuff to editors until you have determined what sort of stuff they lack? To obtain this valuable information (since editors do not often issue circulars defining their wants) the only way is to make a scrutiny of their papers. Go daily, therefore, to a public reading-room, and examine attentively, observantly, the contents of the various publications. Ignore no paper because it has little interest for you personally, or because you have never heard its name before. The more papers you are familiar with, the

wider your field for the disposal of articles. The outside contributor can never tell what paper must serve her turn next. At any moment a subject may occur to her which will suit, say, *The Pottery Gazette and China and Glass Trades Review*, and only *The Pottery Gazette and China and Glass Trades Review*. Study styles and subjects and idiosyncrasies, and count no detail unworthy of attention. The importance to the aspirant of this branch of self-training can scarcely be magnified.

2. Few men and very few women can be trusted to spell correctly every word in common use. I have seen the MSS. of many of the foremost women journalists of the day, and have found orthographic errors in nearly all of them. Of course spelling is not a matter of the highest importance--a certain great English novelist is notoriously incompetent in this respect, and relies upon his printers--but it deserves attention. Bad spelling spoils the appearance of the cleverest article, and raises a prejudice against it in the editorial mind. And not all bad spellers have the ingenuity of Mr. Umbrage of *The Silchester Mirror*, in Mr. J. M. Barrie's novel, *When a Man's Single*:--

   "When Umbrage returned, Billy Kirker, the chief reporter, was denouncing John Milton [the junior reporter] for not being able to tell him how to spell 'deceive.'

   "'What is the use of you?' he asked indignantly, 'if you can't do a simple thing like that?'

   "'Say "cheat,"' suggested Umbrage.

   "So Kirker wrote 'cheat.'"

I think, however, that women have at last learnt to spell words ending in *ieve* and *eive*. They go astray nowadays in *ance* and *ence*; also in *seperate* and *irresistable*, and in the past participles of verbs ending in *it*.

The simplest and best way to cure a case of weak spelling is to hand the dictionary to some wise friend, and ask him or her to question you. A quarter of an hour daily devoted to this treatment will effect a remarkable improvement, even when the patient happens to think there is no room for improvement.

3. Grammar, I suppose, is taught in girls' schools on approved modern principles; nevertheless few women seem to have any acquaintance with it. Yet grammar is not a difficult study, nor a lengthy one, and an understanding knowledge of its principles is of the greatest assistance in the formation of a good literary style. This is a truism: that is why it needs saying again.

   You will find Dr. Richard Morris's *Primer of English Grammar* (Macmillans, *1s*.), with Mr.John Wetherell's *Exercises on Morris's English Grammar* (same publishers and price), very useful, and, though they are small books, quite adequate to your needs. Both can be mastered in a month. The first business is to learn to parse. To parse is "to explain the duty each word performs in a sentence: that is, to tell the relation each word bears to the rest in a sentence:" the definition clearly shows how indispensable to a writer is some skill in parsing. Of course many of the exercises are set obviously for children, but sufficient remain to puzzle the woman of average intelligence. That lady might, for example, have a difficulty in parsing the italicised words in the following: "My cap, having *stuck on* a long *time*, now went *whirling* down the lane." Afterwards comes analysis--the breaking up of a sentence into its component parts--not less urgent than parsing. This branch of the subject is treated well and thoroughly in Mr. Wetherell's book, and his exercises should be worked through conscientiously. Note further, in the same primer, the division relating to syntax, and especially the exercises on pp. 74, 75. The chapter on conjunctions is also of serious importance to women.

4. By "composition," I mean merely the art of writing without transgressing the rules of grammar and kindred canons by which all writers agree to be bound. The higher matter of "style" will be treated in the next chapter.

   The best book on this subject is Professor Nichol's *English Composition* (Macmillan's, 1s.). It is small, but it omits no point on which beginners are likely to err. Women should give particular attention to the following:--

   False concords, p. 22.

   Purity in the use of words, p. 33.

   Want of discrimination between synonyms, p. 39.

   Carelessness as to the meaning of sentences, p. 42.

   The use of relatives, p. 52. Professor Nichol most truthfully says: "The most fertile source of confusion in English is a slovenly use of relatives."

   Arrangement, p. 63.

   For guidance as to punctuation, study *Stops*, by Paul Allardyce (F. Fisher Unwin, 1s.). No book, however, could possibly deal with every point likely to arise under our wonderful English system of punctuation. It is an excellent plan to read aloud any sentence which presents a difficulty, and to punctuate it according to the pauses made (almost unconsciously) by the voice. This method is well-nigh infallible. If doubt still remains, remember that it is better to punctuate too little than too much.

* * * * *

Concurrently with the study of newspapers, spelling, grammar, and composition, the aspirant must make a practice of writing daily a short interesting description (say five hundred words) of some event or scene personally observed during the day. Nothing should be allowed to interfere with the regularity of this exercise, which is essential, not only for the improvement of style, but also for the sharpening of that faculty of subject-selection so necessary to the journalist. It is idle to say: "Nothing interesting ever happens within *my* ken," There is no event, no scene, but has its interesting aspect. Your business, madam, is to discover that aspect.

* * * * *

It may be well to state here that neither shorthand nor typewriting is requisite to the ultimate success of the journalistic aspirant. The common notion that shorthand is part of the equipment of every journalist is quite wrong. If, however, the aspirant possesses a typewriter and the skill to use it, she will of course be able to get her articles transcribed for nothing.

Chapter V

STYLE

"How can I acquire a good style of writing?"

Pathetic question, invariably asked by the artless beginner!

You cannot *acquire* a good style; only a bad style can be acquired.

It is a current impression that style is something apart from, something foreign to, matter--a beautiful robe which, once it is found, may be used to clothe the nudity of matter. Young writers wander forth searching for style, as one searches for that which is hidden. They might employ themselves as profitably in looking for the noses on their faces. For style is personal, as much a portion of one's self as the voice. It is within, not without; it needs only to be elicited, brought to light.

The one possible way of developing the latent style which has always been yours, is to forget absolutely that such a thing as style exists.

For good style consists in saying exactly what you mean with the utmost clearness and the utmost naturalness: simply that! When you have accomplished so much, you have accomplished good style. In no sense is style of the nature of embroidery, an ornament superimposed: this is what the beginner fails to grasp; she somehow cannot rid herself of the superstition that after the meaning is precisely expressed, something further remains to be done.

I have put clearness and naturalness as the two attributes of good style. Clearness need not be defined. Naturalness will not suffer definition; it depends on the individual, and must be determined by the individual. What is proper for one person may be improper for another. Carlyle was ungraceful with impunity; Lamb could not have been so. We may no more choose our styles than our characters. Style, like character, can, it is true, be trained--strengthened, chastened, refined, rendered shapely; but in essentials it must for ever remain as it originally was. It is the expression, not only of the thoughts immediately to be set down, but of the very man himself, and with the man it will develop. It cannot be invented; it cannot be concocted. It must be a natural growth--watched, tended, fostered, pruned, but after all a natural growth.

* * * * *

To find out, to uncover, one's true style; to lay bare one's self: how is this to be set about? Primarily, by experiment in the way of imitation, which is the commencement of all art. Every great artist--Shakspere, Beethoven, Velasquez, Inigo Jones--has started by imitating the models which he admired and to which he felt drawn. You must do the same. It is the surest and indeed the only way of arriving at one's true individuality.

I do not find it easy to recommend exemplars to the aspirant; so many writers of indubitable greatness have been fatal to their disciples; take the trite instance of Carlyle, whose influence twenty years ago ruined styles innumerable. Shakspere and Congreve, possibly our two supreme prose artists, have styles which, in directness and freedom from mannerism, are well suited to be models for the young journalist; but since they wrote only dialogue, now archaic in many details, it is very difficult for the young journalist to follow them with profit in descriptive work. Among modern writers, Mrs. Alice Meynell has a style unsurpassed in simplicity, fineness, and strength. Nevertheless I hesitate to name her as a model, lest the student, in trying to attain her succinct perfection, should fall into mere baldness. On the whole, my inclination turns towards Huxley's *Essays*. Here you have a style which, though by no means great, possesses every good quality, and has besides no tricks to lead the beginner astray; nothing more adorably fitted to the uses of newspaper work could be conceived. To these might be added the letters of Cowper, and the more popular essays of Matthew Arnold.

Paraphrasing is an excellent practice. Read a passage from the author of your choice; grasp thoroughly its purport, but do not learn it by heart. Then close the book, and endeavour to set down in fresh words the thing you have read. In a few days (not at once) compare your work with the classic. The comparison will induce humility, and humility is the beginning of knowledge. After a period of pure imitation you will begin, at first almost imperceptibly, to diverge into a direction of your own. Then proceed warily, making the curve very gradual.

Never attempt to pass judgment on your writing before it is a week old. Until a reasonable interval has elapsed, it is impossible for you to distinguish between what you had in your mind and what is actually on the paper; the brain, still occupied with the thought to be expressed, unconsciously supplies the omissions and clarifies the obscurities of the written word, which thus seems more satisfactory and convincing than it really is. With the passage of time, the thought fades, and the written expression of it, no longer illuminated by memory, must then stand with you on its intrinsic merits. When thus examining your work, read it aloud: the process will disclose weaknesses of all sorts not previously suspected.

Do not destroy anything which you have written. It is well from time to time to refer to past work. To find that one has progressed is always an encouragement to further effort.

So far generally.

As this book does not happen to be a guide to style, it is impossible here to discuss every point likely to arise during the aspirant's self-education in the art of literary expression. But there are several scarlet sins against which she must be briefly warned.

The worst of them is the sin of using trite expressions--phrases, figures, metaphors, and quotations; such as--not to mince the matter, took occasion to, won golden opinions, the cynosure of all eyes, mental vision, smell of the lamp, read mark learn and inwardly digest, inclines towards, indulge in, it is whispered, staple topic of conversation, hit the happy medium, not wisely but too well, I grieve to say, reign supreme, much in request, justify its existence, lend itself amiably to, choice galore, call for remark, hail with delight; and forty thousand others. The work of some writers is chiefly made up of these hackneyed locutions. Says Schopenhauer, in an illuminative passage which I cull from his clever but uneven essay "On Authorship and Style":--"Everyday authors are only half conscious when they write, a fact which accounts for their want of intellect and the tediousness of their writings: they do not really themselves understand the meaning of their own words, because they take ready-made words and learn them. Hence they combine whole phrases more than words--*phrases banales*. This accounts for that obviously characteristic want of clearly defined thought; in fact, they lack the die that stamps their thoughts, they have no clear thought of their own; and in place of it we find an indefinite, obscure interweaving of words, current phrases, worn-out terms of speech, and fashionable expressions. The result is that their foggy kind of writing is like print that has been done with old type. On the other hand, intelligent people *really* speak to us in their writings, and this is why they are able both to move and to entertain us. It is only intelligent writers who *place individual words together with a full consciousness of their use,* and select them with deliberation."

If you have something to say, instead of accepting the first phrases that present themselves (which are naturally those you have heard the most often, and therefore the tritest), endeavour to express yourself in words of your own individual choice, *selected singly*. When you have put a sentence together, examine each word separately, and unless it can satisfactorily account for its position there, by proving appositeness and either originality or indispensability, then cast it aside. The conscientious performance of this rite will soon give a wonderful freshness and piquancy to your style.

Here I must mention a book invaluable to all writers--a book of which I (as a writer) think so well, that if I might only possess one book and had to choose between this and a Shakspere, I would let the Shakspere go. I refer to Roget's *Thesaurus of English Words and Phrases* (Longman, 10s. 6d.). It is in effect a vast collection of synonyms, divided and subdivided minutely and with precision. When you lack the *mot juste*, turn in the index at the end of the volume to any word which, however distantly, approaches in meaning the one you need but cannot summon; you will find a reference to a laborious and magnificent group of allied words amongst which the desired, the unique word is sure to be discovered. For example, we will suppose you require another word for "difficulty"; consider this list:--

"Nouns. Difficulty, hardness (and nouns formed from similar adjectives); impracticability, &c. (see *impossibility*); tough-, hard-, uphill- work; hard-, herculean-, Augean-task; task of Sisyphus, Sisyphean labour, tough job, teaser, rasper, dead lift.

"Dilemma, embarrassment; perplexity, &c. (see *uncertainty*); intricacy; entanglement; cross fire; awkwardness, delicacy, ticklish card to play, knot, Gordian knot, *dignus vindice nodus*, net, meshes, maze; coil, &c. (see *convolution*); crooked path.

"Nice-, delicate-, subtle-, knotty point; vexed question, *vexata quæstio*, poser, puzzle, &c. (see riddle); paradox; hard-, nut to crack; bone to pick, crux, *pons asinorum*, where the shoe pinches.

"Nonplus, quandary, strait, pass, pinch, pretty pass, stress, brunt; critical situation, crisis; trial, rub, emergency, exigency, scramble.

"Scrape, hobble, slough, quagmire, hot water, hornet's nest; sea-, peck of troubles: pretty kettle of fish; pickle, stew, *imbroglio* mess, ado; false position; set fast, stand; dead,-lock,-set; fix, horns of a dilemma, *cul de sac*; hitch; stumbling block, &c. (see *hindrance*)."

The catalogues of allied adjectives and of allied verbs are even longer than the foregoing.

The Introduction to the *Thesaurus*, by the way, though deserving of study, is a dull and cumbrous piece of work and not necessary to the usefulness of the book.

* * * * *

The sin of using trite expressions is equally common among men and women. There are others which chiefly beset women:--

Undue insistence. I have touched upon this in Chapter II. The remedy is to use superlatives only under compulsion, and to eschew italics and such adverbs as "absolutely," "utterly," "positively."

Wordiness. When you have written a paragraph, examine it carefully with the object of eliminating every word which is not necessary to the expression of the meaning. Be sure that you have not said the same thing twice in different words. Keep watch especially against pleonasms. Let this be your motto: Brevity without baldness.

Undue use of metaphor, simile, and figure. This is a sin to which women are wofully prone. They commit it with glee, and I have often found it a most difficult matter to make them realise the absurdities which result from the practice of it. As an illustration of the ludicrous consequences of unbridled indulgence in metaphor and simile, I quote the following extract (not, however, the work of a woman) from a serious and justly respected newspaper.

"I have gasped in wonder to witness one of Her Majesty's judges forsake--on very insufficient provocation--the gossamer of recreative conversation, to upraise a few monumental, I may say memorable, judgments on the subject of lithography. Now, there are many red rags in the various arts with which to encompass the discomfiture of the Philistine's bull, and the raven will always appropriate the feathers of the peacock and look ridiculous in them; but the rapier enwreathed in the red rag of painting is more readily rushed upon, and plumes of appreciation more wantonly borrowed and grotesquely worn in this walk of art than in any other."

Shun especially mixed metaphors. [Footnote: The most beautiful instance of mixed metaphor I have ever seen occurred in a solicitor's letter, brought to my notice by the clerk to whom it was dictated. It ran thus:--"We go upon the principle that, in order to pull the matter out of the fire, a fourth of a fifth of a loaf is better than no bread, which the terms proposed are."] See the section on figurative language (p. 76) in Nichols' *English Composition*. But do not take Nichols himself as a model; I find him writing thus:--"Avoid an accumulation of little words. The *luggage* of particles is an *impediment* to strong speech and a *jar* in the harmony of style," which is nearly as funny as the funny examples which he quotes.

Chapter VI

THE OUTSIDE CONTRIBUTOR

In Mr. J.M. Barrie's *When a Man's Single* [Footnote: This brilliant novel should be seriously studied by every young journalist. It contains more useful advice to the outside contributor than all the manuals of journalism ever written.] the following homily is delivered by a journalist of experience to a naive and innocent beginner:--

"There are only about a dozen papers in London worth writing for, but I can give you a good account of them. Not only do they pay handsomely, but the majority are open to contributions from anyone. Don't you believe what one reads about newspaper rings. Everything sent in is looked at, and if it is suitable any editor is glad to have it. Men fail to get a footing on the press because--well, as a rule because they are stupid."

This is indeed wisdom. I demur to the first sentence alone. There are to-day (whatever the case ten years ago) many more than a dozen papers in London worth writing for; I should put the number nearer a hundred; papers which pay, if not handsomely, at least adequately, seldom lower than fifteen shillings per thousand, and in some noble instances ascending to two guineas--which is princely. A dozen papers worth writing for in the whole of London! Why, it is scarcely uncommon for a single firm to have control of a dozen reputable publications!

The beginner must, for her encouragement and solace under rebuffs, grasp firmly the fact that the immense majority of London editors are not merely willing but in truth anxious to peruse such manuscripts as she cares to submit to their notice, and to accept them if suitable. The supply of really suitable material of average quality does not often exceed the demand, and the supply of suitable material which can be called distinguished is always less than the demand. This is why the editorial eye keeps a sleepless watch for that long-desired new writer, who may be yourself. Also, the beginner should remember with pride that the Press as a whole relies for much of its freshness and attraction upon the outside contributor. If the stream of unsolicited contributions were suddenly to cease flowing into Fleet Street, the monthlies would find themselves in a predicament; all the weeklies (except certain "class" organs), from the esoteric literary sixpenny to the penny popular with a circulation equal to the population of Glasgow, would be compelled to cast aside dignity, and solicit instead of being solicited; even those pompous creatures, the "great dailies," would feel the pinch, despite their regular services and seething staffs. Let it be your glory, therefore, O outside contributors, that the very existence of the Press, as at present organised, depends upon yourselves.

* * * * *

I have already referred to the necessity of visiting regularly a public news-room. As you progress in the power of composition, so must your knowledge of the "make-up" of all the principal papers increase; for the first is useless without the second. You must, in particular, know intimately the complicated topography of all the daily papers--on what days certain features appear; what length of article is affected by each paper; and the subtle variations of tone which, apart from grosser differences, distinguish one organ from another. You must also be well acquainted with the various editorial notices, and take care, when sending in manuscripts, always to obey the instructions there laid down.

The length of an article is a most important matter and frequently decides its fate. Accordingly, the question of lengths must be thoroughly studied. For a simple example, you must know that a *Globe* "turnover" (the celebrated daily article which occupies the last column on the first page and "turns over" to the second page) must necessarily exceed a thousand words; no article intended for that position, whatever its merit, can have the least chance of acceptance if it falls short of this minimum. Again, the first article in the *Evening Standard* must exactly fill the column, no more and no less.

Do net despise "class" papers, those which appeal only to a particular section of the community--religious, architectural, literary, artistic, and so forth. These papers sometimes experience a difficulty in getting what articles they desire, and indeed it is notorious that the editors of certain of them are often at their wits' end in the search for new treatments of an exhausted subject. The reasons for such a state of affairs are, of course, first, that outside contributors in their blindness pass over these papers, and secondly, that as the subjects are sharply limited, so is the field for copy.

It would be well to buy for reference Sells' *Dictionary of the World's Press* (7s. 6d.), a vast volume containing indexes of all papers, with their addresses, and a quantity of useful information concerning them. *The Literary Year Book* (George Allen, 3s. 6d.), gives a tabular statement (incomplete, but useful so far as it goes) showing the editorial requirements of a number of weekly and monthly organs.

* * * * *

Naturally it is impossible to offer particular advice upon so immense a subject as the selection of topics for articles, but attention is directed to the following three points:--

1. Editors, especially editors of weeklies and monthlies, find it necessary to make their arrangements far in advance of publishing day. Therefore the outside contributor must always look ahead. In March she should have an eye on Midsummer, at Midsummer she should be engrossed by Christmas, and at Christmas that notorious article, "Easter in many Lands," should be approaching completion. It is useless to send in (as so many thoughtless ones do send in) an essay on the New Year just before Christmas, or a seaside dissertation towards the end of July. And this applies not only to the great annual festivals and seasons, but also to all important political, social, and general events whose dates are known beforehand. Take, for an instance, the annual meeting of the British Association. If you send to an editor an anecdotal history of the British

Association only a a few days before the meeting itself, you thereby assume that the editor is depending for his topical articles on chance contributions received at the last moment. Which is patently absurd. Without doubt that editor had arranged his British Association articles a couple of months previously, and it is not improbable that he accepted the suggestions of some outside contributor who had been clever enough to look into the future. It is a good plan to compile for reference a calendar of festivals, seasons, and public events, exactly such as the editor himself must use.

2. Women need not confine themselves to women's subjects. Many women writers seem to think that they are debarred by some defect or limitation of sex from treating topics other than those commonly termed feminine. But there is no reason why a woman should not deal as effectively as a man with general matters. (To argue that, because the male journalist does not usually touch women's affairs without being ridiculous, therefore the converse holds good, is illogical.) I lay stress on this.

3. Do not disdain to write mere paragraphs. The present is an era of paragraphs, and they form a most marketable commodity. Scarcely an editor but is continually gaping for topical paragraphs. Moreover paragraphs are less difficult to write than articles, since they demand less constructive skill; many aspirants can put together a passable paragraph who would fail miserably with an article. Further, they have a better chance of acceptance, *cæteris paribus*, for the reason that editors find them easier to handle. Often an editor declines an

article which he likes, simply because he knows that to use it would involve the re-modelling of an entire issue; a paragraph is more amenable. Lastly, paragraphs are paid for, and just as much as articles they may afford one the encouraging satisfaction of seeing her stuff in print. The beginner, therefore, will do well to begin with paragraph work; articles may follow at a later stage.

* * * * *

Your paragraph or article having been composed, there arises the question of the proper way to copy and dispatch it:--

1. In the majority of instances it is unnecessary to typewrite. Typewriting is somewhat expensive and often inaccurate, and unless you happen to possess your own typewriter, there is no reason why caligraphy should not suffice for your needs. (A few editors, however, insist that all copy submitted shall be typewritten.) Use quarto paper--that is, the size of a sheet of note-paper opened--and only one side of it. Write very plainly, not too small, leaving a wide margin at the left hand, and a good space between the words and between the lines.
2. Fasten the sheets together at the top left hand corner with a paper fastener, the pointed ends of the fastener being at the top. Do not pin the sheets; do not stitch them; whatever else you do, refrain from stitching them all the way down the left hand side, as this process makes it irritatingly difficult to turn them over.
3. Write your name and address not only at the top of the manuscript itself, but also on the back, so that they may be prominent when the manuscript is folded up. Write boldly on the first page the exact length of the article in words.

4. Enclose a stamped and addressed envelope--not a book-post wrapper; manuscripts which see much of the world (and your earlier manuscripts will probably see a very great deal of the world) become damaged and ruinous by travelling in a book-post wrapper. Be sure that the envelope is sufficiently stamped, and be sure also that it is large enough to hold the manuscript.
5. Never send out a dirty or ragged manuscript. The editor is prejudiced by the first sight of such a manuscript, for he knows at once that it has been refused elsewhere.

* * * * *

Her manuscript decently dispatched, the aspirant will feel happy and well satisfied till shortly before the earliest hour possible for its return. Then begins suspense. She will sit awaiting with counterfeit calm the postman. She hears his tread on the pavement outside; he mounts the steps, knocks; there is the gentle concussion of a packet against the bottom of the letter-box. Is it the article returned? She still keeps hope. Even when one day the large envelope, addressed in her own writing, is put into her hands, she says to herself that the editor has only returned it for a few trifling modifications....

Invariably the thing does come back, sooner or later, with some curt circular of refusal. Moodiness and discouragement follow. But it is as wise to be annoyed by editors as to quarrel with the weather. Idle depression must instantly give place to renewed activity. The journalistic instinct, says Noble Simms in *When a Man's Single*, "includes a determination not to be beaten as well as an aptitude for selecting the proper subjects."

If at first you fail--as will certainly be the case; you may sell nothing whatever for twelve months--be quite sure that it is not--

Because there is a conspiracy among editors to suppress talented beginners.

Or because the market is overcrowded.

Or because your manuscripts have not been carefully read.

Or because editors do not know their business.

Try to convince yourself that the true reason is--

Because your stuff has not yet reached the (low) level of merely technical accomplishment which the average editor exacts.

Or because your topics are devoid of interest for any numerous body of persons.

Or because you persist in sending your articles to the wrong papers.

The first defect ought to be remedied speedily. The second is more difficult to deal with, and the third is most difficult. The eradication of these two will necessitate careful and continuous study of journalism in all its manifestations, and nothing but successive defeats will teach you how to be victorious. However, perseverance granted, the hour will come when an article of yours finds its way to the composing room. A day of ecstasy, upon which every disappointment is forgotten and the way forward seems straight and facile!

As soon as you can rely upon selling one article out of four, count it that you are progressing.

* * * * *

As to remuneration, a few papers send out cheques at regular intervals without putting their contributors to any trouble in the matter. Others, and among them some of the best, never pay till a demand is made. Some, including one or two organs of note, never pay till they are compelled to do so. If a remittance is not received during the month following publication, it is advisable to deliver an account, giving the date of appearance, exact title, and number of pages, columns, or inches.

Chapter VII

THE SEARCH FOR COPY

There comes a time when the aspirant, proudly conscious of a certain technical skill in composition and construction, and disheartened by repeated failures, exclaims with petulance: "What *shall* I write about?" She dolefully imagines that the list of feasible subjects is exhausted; her wearied brain refuses any longer to carry on its sterile activities, and despair settles down upon her. This is because her eyes have not been opened to the limitless possibilities for the making of good "copy" which exist on every side. Most probably she has been looking in quite the wrong direction.

When Rob Angus, in *When a Man's Single*, remarks to Rorrison, "And yet I had thirty articles rejected before the 'Minotaur' accepted that one," Rorrison's reply is, "Yes, and you will have another thirty rejected if they are of the same kind. You beginners seem able to write nothing but your views on politics, and your reflections on art, and your theories on life, which you sometimes even think original. Editors won't have that, because their readers don't want it. Every paper has its regular staff of leader-writers, *and what is wanted from the outsider is freshness.* An editor tosses aside your column and a half about evolution, but is glad to have a paragraph saying that you saw Herbert Spencer the day before yesterday gazing solemnly for ten minutes in a milliner's window. Fleet Street at this moment is simply running with men who want to air their views about things in general."

With slight modification the satire applies admirably to women. Perhaps women are not so anxious as men to air their views about things in general (though they are tolerably anxious), but they are certainly too prone to write down vaguely their vague *fancies* about things in general. Fleet Street at this moment (to use Rorrison's expressive phrase) is simply running with women who are writing fanciful essays and not selling them because editors don't want fanciful essays--or indeed any sort of essays.

Let us see this fact clear: editors have little use for essays and they have no use for views (except their own). To gain acceptance essays must be extremely well done, and emphatically they are not stuff for beginners to tackle. Apparently the easiest form of composition in the world, the essay is in truth one of the most difficult. Not much experience is needed to prove this. Yet every woman who aspires to journalism must needs employ her clumsy pen upon essays. "From my Window" is a favourite title with the rank beginner. Charles Lamb might conceivably have written an essay called "From my Window" which would have been a masterpiece--and there is a remote chance that some editor might have accepted it. But then Charles Lamb is dead, and his secret died with him.

* * * * *

Despite the vast number of articles written and printed during recent years, there remains a yet vaster number of articles waiting to be written--even after leaving essays out of account. In fact the more articles written, the more to be written. The field for copy has a resemblance to Klondyke: removal of treasure serves only to bring larger quantities into sight.

Journalism ever grows wider, more comprehensive; the whole history of the profession demonstrates this. In the early years of daily journalism, for example, the sole subjects deemed worthy of a newspaper's attention were politics, money, and the law. Some conservative sheets still endeavour to live up to this ideal, but the circulation and the influence go to those which find no aspect of human existence beneath their notice. Formerly newspapers had a morbid dread of being readable. They have lost that dread now, and those which have lost it most completely, most completely succeed. As with the dailies, so with every other sort of paper. The aim is to be inclusive, satisfying the public curiosity and at the same time whetting it; for the more the public knows, the more it wants to know. And it refuses any longer to make a task of newspaper-reading. It demands that it shall be amused while it is instructed, like a child at a kindergarten.

To make sure that you are availing yourself of the immense possibilities for copy which this extraordinary inquisitiveness on the part of the public has fortunately created, you must cultivate an attitude of mind which is constantly asking the question:--

"Is there copy here?"

This attitude may and must be cultivated to such an extent that instead of vainly searching for subjects, you are at a loss to choose among the multitude of ideas for articles which suggest themselves at every turn of existence.

I will illustrate what I mean.

In the first place, it is necessary to remember that articles are divided into two classes--those which are not topical and those which are. Daily papers subsist almost exclusively upon the latter; other papers require both.

We will take the non-topical articles first. These, since they do not spring naturally from passing events, must be suggested by the occurrences of one's everyday life. Thus:--

You get up in the morning.

"Queer ways of sleeping." For *Tit-Bits* and its class. Material at British Museum.

"My alarum." Humorous.

"How to economise space in a small bedroom." For a women's paper.

"Where some Queens sleep." About the sleeping apartments of sovereigns. Ample material in biographies and periodical literature.

"Does a woman require more sleep than a man?" For the silly season.

"Is breakfast in bed enjoyable?" Ditto.

You walk downstairs.

"Some famous staircases."

"Stair-climbing as a form of indoor exercise."

"How to decorate a staircase inexpensively."

You sit down to breakfast.

"Our newsboy." Humorous.

"Papa at breakfast." Ditto.

"The proper way of making coffee." (There is always a market for this kind of thing.)

"How a cup and saucer are made."

"Should the English breakfast be abolished?"

And so on throughout the day.

I put forward these suggestions, not to be worked out, but merely to indicate how notions for articles should come to life in you. A constant effort to evolve ideas in this way cannot fail to be fruitful, and though most of the ideas will be cast aside as valueless, a few promising ones will remain. On no account abandon good articles because you fear they have been done before. Rorrison said: "Of course they have, but do them in your own way; the public has no memory, and besides, new publics are always springing up."

Topical articles are possibly more shy of suggesting themselves than non-topical, but on the other hand they always have a better chance of acceptance. Notions for these cluster about every event or personage that happens to be in the public eye. Suppose we are in April, and the Covent Garden Opera is to open in a month's time. At such a moment editors are naturally susceptible to articles bearing on the subject. For example:--

"Earnings of operatic stars."

"Whims of operatic stars."

Anecdotes (in paragraphic form) relating to any of the singers engaged. These three could be worked up from files of newspapers, particularly of American newspapers.

"How an opera chorus is trained." Material for this might be obtained from intelligent women-members of the chorus, interviewed on the spot.

Notes on the new operas to be produced.

Notes about composers and conductors.

"The Fortunes of Covent Garden Theatre." A historic-anecdotal article. Material at the British Museum.

Notes about the titled box-holders for the season. Material to be obtained from the theatre officials.

And about ninety-nine similar articles.

In the matter of topical articles, I must quote once more from *When a Man's Single*. Simms told Rob Angus "that when anything remarkable occurred in London he should at once do an article at the British Museum on the times the same thing had happened before." This kind of article, if delivered promptly, almost invariably finds a market; but it must be delivered promptly. Then, of course, there are the fixed and movable feasts--Christmas, Easter, &c.,--for which seasonable articles are required. Seasonable articles about these too trite festivals the editor must have (though he would much prefer to dispense with them), and he accepts the least hackneyed suggestions which offer themselves.

* * * * *

Wide as the field for copy already is, it widens, as I have said, continually. In America it is always somewhat wider than in England, and a perusal of the Sunday editions of the leading New York papers, the *Herald, World, Sun, Journal*, &c. (which may be obtained in London), will not be profitless to the alert student. These huge and flaring productions have objectionable features which are only too obvious, but they are conducted by the cleverest journalists in the world, and the invaluable journalistic instinct is apparent on every page of them. The splendid pertinacity and ingenuity of the

American journalist in wringing copy out of any and every side of existence cannot fail to quicken the pulses of those who are accustomed to the soberer, narrower, sleepier ways of English newspapers. Fleet Street pretends to despise and contemn American methods, yet a gradual Americanising of the English press is always taking place, with results on the whole admirable.

* * * * *

Photography is an aid to the outside contributor. Illustrations always assist an article; sometimes they are sufficient to make an unsaleable article saleable. Many articles are capable of being illustrated by means of the camera, and almost any photographic pictures are capable of being "written round." For example, a series of pictures, with brief letterpress, under the title, "The Strand from dawn to dusk," showing incidents of traffic, such as a horse down, &c., would be easily disposed of to an illustrated weekly; such photographs could be taken instanteously on a bright day without any difficulty whatever.

* * * * *

The foregoing remarks on the search for copy are of course addressed to the aspirant living in London, who possesses immense advantages over her rural sister. She has, chiefly, the British Museum, that blessed fount of universal information, and her first duty must be to apply to the Chief Librarian for a reading ticket. Some time will elapse before she is able to use handily the vast apparatus here placed at her disposal, but she will find the officials benignantly omniscient, and always ready to help the unskilled in research. Also, she must not be shy of going into the world and collecting such facts as she may require, ferreting things out, and refusing to be abashed. So soon as she has contributed to a few papers of standing, she should have some cards engraved with her name, and a list of these papers after the words "Contributor to." Such a card will constitute sufficient credentials on any expedition of enquiry, and will frequently aid her to obtain interviews with "people of importance in their day." Interviews, it need scarcely be said, are most popular with the average editor.

The provincial aspirant is less fortunately placed, though if she resides in a large town with a good public library, she may manage tolerably well. It is the woman sepulchred in a small village who finds herself most severely handicapped. Still, I know instances of women so situated who have gained the position of regular contributors to journals of dignity. Their success has been usually due to specialising on some single topic or group of topics, such as "nature notes," "household affairs," "country occupations," "parochial management," "home handiwork," "village sketches," and so on. There is copy even in a village. A woman afflicted with journalistic ambitions once wrote to an editor complaining that she was out of the world, actually two miles from a shop. "Then write an article," the editor replied, "entitled 'Two miles from a shop.'" She did so; it was accepted and followed by others of a similar kind.

Chapter VIII

THE ART OF CORRESPONDING WITH AN EDITOR

Women contributors are commonly much too fond of corresponding with editors. When the aspirant dispatches the first article, it is quite customary for her to send it under cover of a long epistle (not unfrequently extending to eight pages) in which she gives her personal history in brief, and a short statement of her literary ambitions, including in particular her ambition to contribute to "your excellent paper which I have always admired"; often she adds that though not dependant (so she spells the word) upon her own efforts for a livelihood, she is nevertheless anxious to earn a little money; or it may be that she is in fact thrown upon her own resources, in which case she explains that she has turned to journalism as the readiest means of providing for herself. Sometimes she ventures to hope that the editor will judge her work leniently, since she is only a beginner. Sometimes, with affecting candour, she avows that she does not expect for a moment to be accepted. Sometimes she requests that in case of refusal the editor will advise her where next to send the manuscript. Sometimes she begs for a frank criticism, and if the editor is foolish enough to justify his heartless refusal by such a criticism, she pesters the devoted fellow with another long letter of thanks, in which she timidly suggests that he may be able to assist her further, but hopes that he will not trouble to send any answer unless it is quite, quite convenient to him to do so. He doesn't.

In her pre-occupation, she usually forgets either to write her name and address on the manuscript or to enclose stamps; occasionally she omits even to stamp her own letter.

* * * * *

Let this be your rule: Don't write to an editor. He has an objection to both reading letters and answering them; he thinks he does enough when he peruses your manuscript. A good article requires no explanation; it should be its own commentary. Be content, therefore, simply to put your article in an envelope with another envelope, and dispatch it. The editor needs not to be told that it is sent for publication if suitable and for return if unsuitable. And he does not care a pin what are your ambitions and your circumstances; or whether this is your "very first" or your ten thousandth effort; whether you have written in the flush of health or on your dying couch; whether you are starving or beautifully rich. What are these facts to him? They do not in the least affect the value of the article. If it pleases him, he accepts; if not, he refuses. He is scarcely Adviser-in-Chief to the Literary Ladies of Great Britain, nor yet the Charity Organisation Society. He has no interest in you. What interests him is his circulation, his influence, his advertisement department.

The editorial notices of a few papers state that the title and scope of an article must be submitted before the article itself. This is absurd, and in most cases you are safe in ignoring the regulation. An article cannot be judged by its title and a *resumé* of it, and there is no doubt that editors who enforce such a rule often decline to see articles which would have suited them.

If for any special reason a letter should be essential, make it brief, explicit, and formal; spend as much care over the letter as you have given to the article which it is to cover. See that it contains no superfluous words, and see that it is correctly spelt; some letters aren't.

When a series of articles is in contemplation or a novel departure to be suggested, it sometimes happens that a rather elaborate explanation is necessary. Do not send such an explanation in writing until you have demonstrated the impossibility of seeing the editor in person.

Now editors do not like being seen, and certainly they do not like being seen by the casual contributor. Despite the fact that this persevering person is indispensable to them and often their best friend, they fall into the habit of regarding the casual contributor as their natural enemy, against whom warfare is to be waged. It is ridiculous, but it is true. So be it. Accept the situation, and fight for yourself, taking your advantage where you can, and casting away scruples of punctilio. By actually seeing an editor you gain a double advantage. For in the first place it is much more difficult for him to refuse *viva voce* (especially to a woman [Footnote: I by no means suggest that a woman should exploit her femininity in order to gain points against a man.]) than by letter, and in the second place a personal explanation of a scheme is likely to be much more effective than a written one. Therefore resolve to see your editor face to face.

That editors are invisible is taken for granted only by the inexperienced. Without doubt editors love to surround themselves with an atmosphere of mystery, aloofness, and sovereignty, but in truth they are human beings, and may be so treated. The invisibility of editors is mainly a legend. If you call at a newspaper office and, presenting your card, ask in a firm voice to see the editor, the probability is that you will see him, or some one else clothed with authority. You may be requested to state the nature of your business, in which case you will make the nature of your business as vague and enticing as possible. Possibly the editor, if he is timid, will invent the story that he is engaged; possibly he may really be engaged; in either case you will ask for an appointment, or wait; a personal interview is worth waiting for. If you are refused an appointment and also told that to wait would be useless, say that you will call to-morrow or the next day in the hope of the editor being then disengaged. In any event, be pertinacious; and do not fear to worry the man. By pertinacity you will eventually see him.

Having at last got sight of your editor, treat him considerately. Since you have conquered you can afford to show mercy. Explain yourself tersely, and let your visit be brief. Strive to impress by your directness and business-like thought and action.

Chapter IX

NOTES ON THE LEADING TYPES OF PAPERS

In a previous chapter I have emphasised the urgency of examining with care and regularity all the principal papers. Nothing is more important to the outside contributor than a thorough comprehension of their various policies and their essential differences. Many beginners, with a quite creditable literary technique, render all effort futile by omitting to study what I may call the *characters* of the publications to which they offer MSS. They know papers (except the one or two which they happen to read for pleasure) merely by name. They may by chance have some dim notion, gathered from hearsay, of the aim and spirit of this paper or that--but accurate, direct information concerning these things, they possess none. Having written an article, they send it to the first paper whose name enters their heads, without giving a single thought to the question of suitability. By such beginners the *Standard*, the *Sun*, and the *Morning Advertiser* are recognised merely as so many dailies, the *Saturday Review*, *Tit-Bits*, and the *Bazaar* merely as so many weeklies, and the *Strand*, *Macmillan's Magazine*, and the *Fortnightly* merely as so many monthlies; and no doubt when their stuff has been refused by the *Standard,* they blithely forward it to the *Sun*, and so on.

Since the early failures of every aspirant are without doubt largely due to the neglect of this branch of journalistic learning, let me once more lay stress on the fact that every paper differs from every other paper in its needs--in what it demands from the outside contributor. Each paper has its own public, its own policy, its own tone, its own physiognomy, its own preferences, its own prejudices. These must be studied--as one would study a subject like zoology. And as in zoology, to acquire a useful knowledge, it is necessary to classify. The press divides itself naturally into a few distinctive groups, an acquaintance with whose characteristics will form the best, indeed the only, foundation for that wide, detailed erudition ultimately to be obtained through years of experience and observation. Of these groups I will briefly mention the most important.

* * * * *

Perhaps of all the different kinds of papers, that most useful to the beginner is the "popular weekly" class, chiefly represented by *Tit-Bits, Answers, Pearson's Weekly, Cassell's Saturday Journal*, and *Success*. These papers pay liberally and promptly (one or two of them before publication), and they do not exact from the contributor a high literary standard. Their matter falls into two main divisions: articles beginning with "How"--broadly, "How the other half lives;" and articles enumerating curious facts and incidents--for example, "Peers who have become Cabmen." If you can evolve novel and striking subjects, and have the patience to collect such information as may be necessary to work the subjects out, you may fairly rely upon gaining entrance sooner or later to the columns of these papers, however elementary your technique. Here is also a busy market for short melodramatic stories--stories for which "action" and a certain ingenuity of plot are the only essentials. Do not imagine that the editors of this sort of periodical are easily pleased. Although they care nothing for the graces of style, they know precisely what they want, and they insist on getting it.

Next to the popular penny weeklies as prey meet for the aspirant, I name the three "Gazettes," the *Pall Mall*, the *Westminster*, and the *St. James's*. These--the first two especially--make a point of their hospitality to the outside contributor. They appeal of course to a cultured class, and they are catholic in their tastes--ready for anything provided it is topical and well done. They pride themselves on being literary, and therefore good style is essential. In this particular, and also in their habits of returning rejected MSS. with promptness, and of paying regularly without demanding the delivery of an account, they differ from most of the penny morning papers. With them may be bracketed the *Globe* and the *Evening Standard*, both celebrated in Grub Street for a regular daily un-editorial article, to which I have referred in Chapter VI. When you have contributed a "turnover" to the *Globe*, you may congratulate yourself. The *Evening Standard* article has less pretensions.

Save as receptacles for short stories of a lurid inferior kind, the halfpenny evening papers have little interest for the outside contributor. The *Echo* is an exception, showing a fondness for short, quiet, topical articles of a rather serious nature.

Among morning papers, the most attractive to the outside contributor is the *Daily Mail*, one of the best-edited newspapers in the world. The *Daily Mail* does not ask itself on receiving an unsolicited contribution: "Is it our custom to publish things of this kind"? No, it scorns precedent and is always anxious for novelty. It demands absolute freshness, a great deal of *verve*, and the strictest brevity. It makes a feature of very short interviews and articles on topics of the hour. On its seventh page, under the title "The Daily Magazine," room is usually found for matter of a general nature--glorified *Tit-Bits* confections. If the *Daily Mail* has a weakness, it is for statistical articles of an international character, illustrated by ingenious diagrams--articles in which Great Britain by hook or by crook is made to surpass and outvie every other country.

Another halfpenny morning paper, *The Morning*, has burst the fetters of precedent and usage, and willingly considers every suggestion of originality. Its methods are those of New York and frankly sensational.

The penny morning papers are difficult of access, relying chiefly on bands of regular contributors. The least hide-bound are the *Daily Chronicle* and the *Daily News*. On Saturday the former has a women's page, for which it accepts outside contributions with some freedom. The *Daily News* has a reputation for humorous articles dealing with the domesticities.

Of the illustrated sixpenny weeklies, *Black and White* and the *Sketch* are usually ready to consider short stories, dialogues, interviews, and light articles, the *Sketch* being the more exigent of the two. The *Illustrated London News* and the *Graphic* depend for matter upon their own staffs and regular correspondents, and I believe that neither accepts any fiction from outsiders. To the politico-literary weeklies, *Saturday Review*, *Speaker*, and *Spectator*, the aspirant need not turn her ambitious eye. They are fastidious; they demand advanced technique, and moreover they touch subjects with which women are not often conversant. Of the three, the *Speaker* is the least exclusive.

With the vast hordes of religious papers (it is stated that several hundred are published in London alone) I shall make no attempt to deal. But it may be well to say that many of them pay very badly and many of them do not pay at all. The best, speaking from a journalistic point of view, is the *British Weekly*, a Nonconformist journal which prints all sorts of things, and which is edited with brilliant skill; unfortunately it has the bad habit of not returning rejected articles.

As regards the comic weekly press, not much falls to be said. It may be separated into three divisions. First, *Punch* (threepence), which for several decades has stood, and still stands, quite alone. It is usual to say that *Punch* has of late years been steadily losing its reputation, but the truth of the statement seems at least doubtful; and however this may be, indubitably *Punch* is yet the foremost comic weekly. Though it depends in the main upon a regular staff, its doors are not locked against the outside contributor. Second, *Judy* (recently edited by a woman), *Fun*, *Moonshine*, and *Pick-Me-Up* (one penny). Like *Punch*, all these papers, except *Pick-Me-Up*, are noticeably conservative in their policies, and continue to move in the old grooves. They do not, I imagine, offer much opportunity to the outside contributor. *Pick-Me-Up* devotes itself to the humour of the music-hall, and is probably not largely beholden to women for its sprightliness. Third, the halfpenny organs of wit, represented by *Comic Cuts*, and twenty other sorts of *Cuts*. If a woman considers herself destined for the comic press, her wisest course is to collaborate with an artist. A joke may be the best and most original joke in the world, but it will not have a very safe chance of acceptance unless it is illustrated. The illustration *per se* may be without talent; no matter; mediocre pictures have certainly been instrumental in selling innumerable jokes. And as with jokes, so with "skits," satires, and parodies: the writer must combine with the artist if success is to be reached.

Monthly magazines divide themselves into three classes:--First, the purely popular,--*Strand, Ludgate, Pearson's, Windsor, Woman at Home, Lady's Realm*, &c. Second, the high-class general,--*Blackwoods', Pall Mall, Macmillans' Cornhill, Longmans'*, &c. Third, the reviews,--*Nineteenth Century, Contemporary, Fortnightly, National*, and *Westminster*. Of these three classes, the aspirant is likely to succeed best with the second, since the first demands names of renown, and the third either expert knowledge, scholarship, or high technique.

I have left to the last the women's papers, which are, in the natural order of things, written chiefly by women. It is of course to be expected that women-aspirants should turn first to women's papers, of whose characteristics they should certainly make a special and minute study, but at the same time I must repeat the warning already given against the habit of dealing only with subjects interesting to or connected with the female sex. Women's papers are sharply divided into two classes--those which appeal to women of education and breeding, and those which appeal to women of a lower social status. To the former group belong the *Queen*, the *Lady's Pictorial*, the *Gentlewoman* (sixpence), *Hearth and Home* and the *Lady* (threepence), and *Woman* (one penny). To the latter belong *Home Chat*, *Home Notes*, and their countless imitators.

The beginner must bear in mind the essential differences between these two groups, which, in catering for quite different tastes, necessarily follow widely divergent policies. Both groups pay reasonably well, and it may be said that all women's papers of any reputation whatever give a considerate ear to the outside contributor. The sixpennies, having what amounts to unlimited room, offer to the aspirant a spacious and delightful field.

Chapter X

"WOMAN'S SPHERE" IN JOURNALISM

There are certain departments of journalism which women have always had, and probably will always have, to themselves: I mean the departments comprising fashion, cookery and domestic economy, furniture, the toilet, and (less exclusively) weddings and what is called society news. It is unlikely that men will ever seriously compete with women in the business of supplying the stuff which women as a sex are supposed to read. My own belief is that men could deal very capably with these subjects, or most of them, if they chose to assume the task; but there happens to be a superstition that such matters are beyond a man's scope; men accept the superstition, and leave them alone. Hence the distinctive "woman's sphere" in journalism.

Now almost all the work falling within this sphere is done badly--with a lack of technical skill which can only be described as shameful. I have argued (in Chapter II.) that the defect is attributable to the early training which women receive. A further explanation lies in the fact that, in their particular field, they are never stimulated to improvement by the sight of better performances than their own; the result, viewed dispassionately, is deplorable.

In the first place, nearly all women's work dealing with feminine subjects is in a special degree disfigured by slipshod writing. This is particularly true of fashion articles, which are on the whole worse written even than police reports in country newspapers. Of the scores of fashion articles appearing week by week in journals of standing, not five per cent. would pass muster as the work of men. I take up, for an example, one of the "great London dailies," containing a short signed contribution by a journalist whose fame as a chronicler of modes is unrivalled, a lady who earns the wage of a Cabinet Minister, and has indeed arrived at the highest places in her profession; and I find in the article the following--shall I call them?--lapses from the rectitude of sound writing.

Hackneyed phrases and quotations:--

"Read, mark, learn, and inwardly digest."

"Inclines towards the portly."

"*De rigueur.*"

"Hold on our affections."

"Ignore the charms of."

Strange word:--

"Becomingness."

Bad punctuation:--

"So that such a jacket be cut well and worn by a woman of fairly slim proportions round the waist and hips it will be exceedingly successful, but she who inclines towards the portly should rigidly ignore the charms of the jacket with the belt." Unless this sentence has a comma after "well," it bears a meaning quite different from what the writer intended; it needs also a comma after "hips" and a semicolon after "successful."

Words wrongly used:--

"It is one of the *earnest* principles of my faith to commend fashion." A principle cannot be earnest, and faith cannot be an action. The writer probably means that she sincerely thinks it her duty to commend fashion.

"There are only two hats *well* worn in Paris just now--this style and the small velvet toque trimmed with a group of plumes." For "well," read "largely" or "extensively." Note the other fault in this sentence.

Wrong or clumsy constructions, laxity in the use of metaphors, &c.:--

"[We may] read, mark, learn, and inwardly digest their different charms." Fancy reading or learning or digesting a charm!

"I have no objection to the lion lying down with the lamb--the Persian lamb--or rather, I should say, to the sable being allied to this fur, or to the combination of black caracule, or sable with ermine; any two furs, or indeed three furs, put together, I recognise as appropriate and elegant, but the frivolous working of furs with coloured satins and silks now obtaining the affections of the many is not at all to my taste." To comment on this piece of composition would be wicked.

"There is a great fancy shown by the authorities this year *to* elaborate furs." In English one says "*take* a fancy *to*" but "*show* a fancy *for*."

"*It is* small wonder that the fashion has obtained *such* a hold on our affections, because *it is so* becoming if *it is* not overdone."

"A single row of white pearls next the fair or even dark throat of a woman has always a beneficial effect upon her complexion." Has a woman then two throats?

"And talking about a beneficial effect upon a woman's complexion, let me mention once again the exceeding *becomingness* of the new shades of blue, these being rather of the sugar-paper order of blue, but a little lighter in colour perhaps, yet having *that* vivid tone about *it*. *This* is freely mixed with dark blue, the lighter shade being used for *making* trimmings to bodices, or indeed *to make* an entire bodice, while the dark cloth forms the skirt and coat. The hat which completes *it* will take every shade of blue." Observe particularly the two "its" and the "this," neither of which refers properly to any substantive.

So much for the craftsmanship of one of our most celebrated women-journalists! When such a person, writing over her own name in the columns of a renowned and powerful paper, may thus brazenly ignore the elementary principles of composition, it may be guessed what latitude of carelessness and error is allowed to obscurer performers in obscurer sheets.

* * * * *

It is not only in the apparently trivial but really important details of style that women's work falls short, but in qualities even more vital. Fashion, to refer again to that branch of journalism, is a complicated and difficult subject, requiring for its adequate treatment the utmost orderliness and lucidity. Yet fashion articles are seldom arranged with any skill, and seldom lucid. The subject is usually handled after a haphazard method resulting in misty paragraphs of which often not even the writers could explain the meaning. It is said that men cannot understand fashion articles. Certainly they cannot, but the fault is not theirs. Over and over again I have heard expert fashion-journalists confess that they had failed to comprehend the writings of their colleagues. If articles on dress were properly done, men could understand, though they might not be interested in them.

Fashion gives the widest scope for the journalist's art. The constant change, the bewildering variety of it, offer opportunities for descriptive and critical work which, if they were seized, might result in articles as interesting, as accomplished, as distinguished, as any in the literary reviews. But these opportunities are uniformly missed.

Cookery, that is to say practical cookery, gives fewer opportunities than fashion for the display of merely literary skill. It is a subject which demands from the journalist clearness and thoroughness. The average cookery article may be passably clear so far as it goes, but it is rarely thorough, and so it fails in usefulness. Writers upon cookery in women's papers have been content, without thinking upon what is really wanted, to follow the methods of cookery books, ignoring the truism that cookery books, by reason of their omissions and silences, are valuable only to efficient cooks, who stand in no deep need of them. It is to the inexperienced cook that cookery articles are designed to appeal, and therefore they should be exhaustive, describing processes exactly, measuring quantities with precision, taking nothing for granted, leaving nothing to the imagination. That cookery articles, even if read, are certainly not acted upon, is proved by the monotony of the suburban dinner. And they are not acted upon because the reader finds them incomplete, "sketchy," and superficial.

It would be possible to take all the other subjects coming within "woman's sphere" in journalism, and to show that women have failed in the treatment of them to reach even a moderate standard of competence. Look, for another instance, at the reports of weddings and society entertainments, all done after one execrable model, dull and perfunctory.

* * * * *

I bring this general indictment in order that the eyes of the aspirant may be opened to the opportunities which await her. A brilliant future lies before the woman who will devote to these neglected women's subjects skilled craftmanship and the enthusiasm of an artist, of which surely they are as worthy as anything else in journalism. At present it seems as if the women who write for women are content to remain all their lives mere amateurs of the pen; the one who first puts herself to the trouble of becoming an expert may rely upon making a sensation in the world of editors.

Chapter XI

CONCLUSION

It is not part of my scheme to deal with newspaper offices, and so disturb the illusions of the aspirant concerning the "glamour" of those places. To those who are outside them and would fain be inside, a newspaper office is a retreat where, amid cigarette smoke and the rumour of continual event, clever people write what they like when they like, while others, only one degree less gifted, correct, by means of cabalistic signs, proofs, with the rapidity of lightning and the omniscience of gods, exchanging at intervals brilliant repartee with the beings who write. Round these are supposed to hover boys, compositors, porters, famous contributors and timid aspirants, and in the underground distance is the roar and vibration of vast steam machines which disgorge papers more quickly than one can count.

The reality is perhaps different from this picture--how different the aspirant will realise when she has at last obtained a position in an office. Having obtained such a position, she may congratulate herself that the most trying part of the apprenticeship is over. Henceforward she will be among those who can put her in the right way. She will no longer need the assistance of a handbook; it is only the unattached beginner, working (so pathetically) without guidance and in the dark, who needs that.

One thing, however, may be said about the newspaper office. It is as strictly a place of business as a draper's shop or a bank. Many women-journalists fail to recognise this fact. They do not see that in an office the relations of people must be first and foremost official; that social considerations, and even considerations of animal comfort, must be put aside in order that Business may have a clear road.

I have met in newspaper offices the sprightly woman who martyrises herself because she must work in a room with other women whose dullness and primness jar on her vivacities; the woman who is aggrieved because winter is warmed for her by a gas stove instead of an open fire; the woman who feels insulted because male associates do not accord her the elaborate ritual of deference to which she has been accustomed in drawing-rooms; the woman who arrives late because she is tired, and blandly offers to "make up the time at night;" the woman who says, "I forgot to do so and so, I'm *so* sorry," and stands like a spoiled child smilingly expectant of forgiveness; and other women of a similar kind.

A vast number of women engaged in journalism, I verily believe, secretly regard it as a delightful game. The tremendous seriousness of it they completely miss. On no other assumption can the attitude of many women-journalists towards their work be explained. Therefore, my final words to the outside contributor, as I leave her on the threshold of an office, are these: Journalism is not a game, and in journalism there are no excuses.